TEARS *of* SILENCE

TEARS *of* SILENCE

A MEDITATION

JEAN VANIER

PHOTOGRAPHS BY
JONATHAN BOULET-GROULX

FOREWORD BY
PARKER J. PALMER

ANANSI

This edition published in 2014 by
House of Anansi Press Inc.
110 Spadina Avenue, Suite 801
Toronto, ON, M5V 2K4
Tel. 416-363-4343
Fax 416-363-1017
www.houseofanansi.com

Distributed in Canada by
HarperCollins Canada Ltd.
1995 Markham Road
Scarborough, ON, M1B 5M8
Toll free tel. 1-800-387-0117

Distributed in the United States by
Publishers Group West
1700 Fourth Street
Berkeley, CA 94710
Toll free tel. 1-800-788-3123

House of Anansi Press is committed to protecting our natural environment. As part of our efforts, the interior of this book is printed on paper that contains 100% post-consumer recycled fibres, is acid-free, and is processed chlorine-free.

18 17 16 15 14   1 2 3 4 5

Library and Archives Canada Cataloguing in Publication

Vanier, Jean, 1928–, author
     Tears of silence / by Jean Vanier ; photographs by Jonathan Boulet-Groulx.

Poems.
Edition includes a new preface by Jean Vanier and a foreword by author and education activist Parker J. Palmer.
Issued in print and electronic formats.
ISBN 978-1-77089-834-9 (bound).—ISBN 978-1-77089-835-6 (html)

     I. Boulet-Groulx, Jonathan, 1984– photographer II. Title.

PS8593.A55T4 2014   C811'.54   C2014-902724-9
                                                 C2014-902725-7

Library of Congress Control Number: 2014938785

Book design: Alysia Shewchuk
All photographs by Jonathan Boulet-Groulx

We acknowledge for their financial support of our publishing program the Canada Council for the Arts, the Ontario Arts Council, and the Government of Canada through the Canada Book Fund.

Printed and bound in Canada

CONTENTS

FOREWORD

By Parker J. Palmer

Years ago, I met a woman I'll call Maureen who had a young daughter I'll call Rebecca. Rebecca had a severe developmental disability and could do very little for herself. So Maureen, a single mother, had to live two lives, leaving her with little or no time for what most of us would call "a life of her own."

Few people understood that Maureen had the best kind of life one could have — a life of self-giving love, expressed through unconditional love for a child who would never be considered "attractive" or "useful" or "successful" by society's standards. Those standards were irrelevant to Maureen. She loved Rebecca not for what she could achieve but for who she was: a human being precious to the earth, a cherished child of God.

Maureen surrounded Rebecca with the kind of love that touched everyone she met, including me. I grew up in an achievement-oriented community where many looked at life as a competition and suffered from the sense that they did not have what it takes to "win." But in Maureen's presence — in the presence of a heart that embraced people for who they were, not what they could do — I felt free, blessed, whole, at home in my own skin, and at peace in my soul.

The gift Maureen gave me — the gift of unconditional love — is one I need as much today at age seventy-five as I did when I was young. We spend so much of our lives being treated as a means to someone else's end, valued only if we are useful to others. And, sad to say, we often treat others as means to our ends. In a culture where we are regarded as human *doings* rather than human *beings*, it's no wonder that so many of us walk around feeling wounded, afraid that if accident or illness or the diminishments of age were to prevent us from achieving, there would be no love left for us. If people like me feel wounded — people who are, as they say, "fully functional" and have been declared "winners in the game of life" — how much deeper are the wounds of those who live on the margins of our society because of developmental disabilities, poverty, abuse, and neglect?

Amid all this suffering, there are no adequate words to give thanks for the shining work and witness of Jean Vanier and L'Arche. For fifty years, this great man and the international federation of residential communities he founded have been reminding us that people are infinitely valuable for who they are, not for what they can do. *Tears of Silence* amplifies this message with Jean Vanier's moving words and with the powerful photographs of co-author Jonathan Boulet-Groulx.

If you don't know about L'Arche, I urge you to learn more by visiting their website, where you will find these introductory words:

> Founded by Jean Vanier in France in 1964, L'Arche communities bear witness to the reality that persons with intellectual disabilities possess inherent qualities of welcome, wonderment, spirituality, and friendship. We make explicit the dignity of every human being by building inclusive communities of faith and friendship where people with and without intellectual disabilities share life together. L'Arche exists to strengthen our local communities, welcome more people into our life and work, engage in advocacy on behalf of those often on the margins of society, and to raise awareness of the gifts of persons with intellectual disabilities.

There's a story behind the words "founded by Jean Vanier in 1964" that reveals the heart of L'Arche. Jean did not create a new project or program or institution in 1964. Instead, he simply invited Raphael Simi and Philippe Seux, two men with disabilities, to leave the institutions where they resided to live with him at his residence in Trosly-Breuil, France. So from the outset, L'Arche has been a *family*, and has created homes and "a place in the sun" for thousands of people who would otherwise be among the neglected and rejected of our world, barely able to survive, let alone feel embraced by others. L'Arche has brought together many Maureens with many Rebeccas in a way that offers comfort to hearts lost in pain and light to a world lost in darkness.

Jean Vanier is one of the world's great teachers of love of the most important sort, love for those who are "the least among us." And he is the best kind of teacher, one who teaches not merely with his words but with his witness. As you read *Tears of Silence*, you are reading words that have become flesh, incarnated in the lives of all who have heard and accepted the invitation to give and receive unconditional love, words that invite the reader — you and me — to embody this kind of love in our own lives and relationships.

Thomas Merton once described God as "mercy within mercy within mercy." When I look around this suffering world for evidence of this God who multiplies mercy without end, I always recall with deepest gratitude the life and work of Jean Vanier and the international network of L'Arche communities he has helped develop over the past half-century.

Few of us who read this book will feel called or able to join a L'Arche community. But all of us can join in the spirit of love that animates this redemptive movement. We can learn to listen for the "tears of silence" that are being shed around us every day, and do whatever we can to work toward that blessed day when, as promised in the Book of Revelation, "every tear shall be wiped away."

Parker J. Palmer, Founder and Senior Partner of the Center
for Courage & Renewal, and author of nine books, including
Healing the Heart of Democracy, The Courage to Teach,
A Hidden Wholeness, *and* Let Your Life Speak

PREFACE

By Jean Vanier

Tears of Silence was first published in 1970, just six years after I started to live with Raphael Simi and Philippe Seux, both of whom had been locked up in a dismal and violent institution for people with intellectual deficiencies. The tears of this book were the cry of my heart faced with the pain and humiliation of so many people abandoned in terrible institutions or on the streets. They were also the cry of anger, which rose up within me, at the indifference of a world blindly seeking more wealth, power, and acclaim. Yet the tears deeply belong to those who then and still today cry silently in the despair of their hearts not daring to hope that they will ever be heard.

Since the creation of the first community of L'Arche, fifty years have flown by and our communities are now spread throughout the world. And yet, too many people in too many countries remain oppressed, humiliated, and rejected. There is so much injustice everywhere. My tears and anger remain, even if the righteous anger has been tempered by the consciousness of how hard we all find it to open up to others who are different and in need, and to let ourselves be transformed by the other. When we remain locked into our own cultures and certitudes, and our need to become more powerful and wealthy, we also remain oblivious to the weak of our world. It is not easy to move out from the closed realities of our groups to discover the beauty of our human family, which in so many ways surpasses all the differences of culture and religion.

We are so deeply divided. So many remain locked up in depression, whether that be depression rooted in loneliness and rejection or in the surfeit of security and comfort. The road to liberation and transformation is long for each one of us. Over the past fifty years I have become aware of the danger of judging and so condemning the other and hardening our differences. Yet compassion and indignant anger are still needed today if we are to break out of the fetters that bind us and to embody our tears in relationships that bring new life to all.

Where do we find the courage to let ourselves be challenged and transformed so that we might rise up as messengers of peace and unity? I pray and hope that this new edition with the telling and moving photos taken by Jonathan may encourage more and more people to risk crossing the barriers that separate us, and to risk becoming friends with those we have rejected, so that they too might rise up in hope.

INTRODUCTION

By Jonathan Boulet-Groulx

It is said that a photograph can replace a thousand words and that a single word can conjure a thousand images. In a way, this is what *Tears of Silence* also does — it is a collection of words and photographs that tell a story. A single story can show us the roots of our lives.

This book is being brought back into the world because I had the privilége of meeting M. Vanier for the first time three years ago. The idea for the reissue of this edition came after that meeting. More importantly, it was also the birth of the collaboration between M. Vanier, the founder of L'Arche, and myself, a very young photographer who discovered through L'Arche that his passion lay in capturing people and their stories.

Every photograph you encounter in this book is a story; each represents the many faces of life, love, struggle, and power. They are part of a lifelong personal project to discover how human fragility can help us become better citizens, better brothers and sisters, better friends, lovers, caregivers, dreamers, and decision-makers, and how fragility can make us better at being who we are using the gifts we have. When I say fragility, I'm referring to the facet of our personalities that makes us feel vulnerable to others. We have learned to hide our vulnerability and to be ashamed of weakness, disability, illness, emotion, old age or youth, yet fragility helps us discover what lies inside and it is a part of who we are. Our response to the fragility of others, as individuals and collectively, can be rejection or inclusion. The choice will always be ours: to close ourselves off or to open up.

If I have decided to make fragility the central focus of my work, it is because I believe this theme is infinitely more unifying and contemporary than we realize. An inclusive society, one that gives all of its citizens a place, becomes a more human society. It's an aspect of humanity that we are desperately short of today, evolving as we are towards a world where individualism seems to be the chief sign of success.

It's hard to look in someone's eyes and see that they are suffering. It screams at your heart that maybe, just maybe, you could be doing something. It is frightening and powerful, and often we feel too little, too frail, or powerless to do anything. Yet something in us screams back, a voice inside that doesn't want to let go of love and compassion. Indignation and courage compel us to rise up. We all need to keep rising up if we want a better world.

Then what should we be doing? Just a step in the right direction. Crossing the road to meet others, letting ourselves be touched by others. Something as simple as a smile and a nod. The rest will happen by itself.

We have something to learn from each other about the art of welcoming, acceptance, and life in a community. Maybe we can reveal to each other that difference, fragility, and beauty are not always found where we might imagine.

TEARS *of* SILENCE

A MEDITATION

Our lives are fleeting moments in which are found both the seeds of peace, unity, love and also the seeds of war, dissension, and indifference. When will we rise and awaken to the desire to water and to tend to the seeds of peace, unity, and love? Who will dare?

With prayerful listening, wise encouragement, and mutual forgiveness, we can walk together on the path towards peace. Through our relationships with each other and with God, who holds us close in our poverty, we can be transformed, healed, and brought into the fullness of life. Together with the most marginalized of the world, we can become a sign of hope for humanity.

This book is dedicated to all the faces that are shown here, faces and people who represent you and me, all those who are fearful, and all those who aspire to universal brotherhood and sisterhood.

I grieve to speak of love and yet not love as I might.
I ask forgiveness of the many I have wounded
and of the many I have passed without seeing their wounds.
Pray for me, my brothers and sisters.

How many times
has an encounter revealed barriers
rigid refusal
within me
heart of stone
heart of stone
unable to listen
I fear
and hurry by
who can liberate me from myself?

The person who clings desperately to security and normality
to everyday habits, work, organization, friends,
family
closed off
no longer lives.

More than security and normality,
life needs
adventure
risk
dynamic activity
friendship
self-giving
tenderness
prayerful listening
presence of others.

On the path of our lives
there are sometimes obstacles
blocking our way
when these overwhelm us
we are fatigued and discouraged,
we sit and weep
deflated
unable to go forward
unable to go back
or if some failure has dampened our spirit
an unfaithful friend
failure in exams
in work or in relationship
we no longer feel that blossoming dynamism
we carry our bodies like lumps of lead
we slip into a world of discouragement
apathetic
listless
then, change comes
winter melts into spring
we meet a friend
we take a rest or a holiday
forces awaken in our bodies and our spirits
life seems to spring forth once more within us
as the morning sun
calm
unfaltering
steadfast.

Others fall,
sink into sadness,
struggle to rise
then fall again too quickly
meeting obstacle after obstacle
becoming deflated...depressed...downhearted...
crushed
life no longer blossoms
the joy of living has vanished,
maybe never was,
quickly being sucked
from depression
into despair
from sadness
into misery
isolated
alone.

The person
overcome with misery
crushed
without hope of new life
surrounded
by obstacles and difficulties
no desire
no motivation
no will to live
closed off
isolated
alone.

We human beings
are marvelous and mysterious
when called forth
with compassion and tenderness
through attentive presence and prayerful listening
strength
hope
surge up from within
giving life
a blossoming of quiet energy.

Treated with recognition
as a fellow human,
in spite of my brokenness
in spite of my poverty,
there emerges
capacity for creativity
generosity

deep attention
concern
work
a sense of wonderment
a taste of the infinite
unceasing
evolving
deepening
creating
calling.

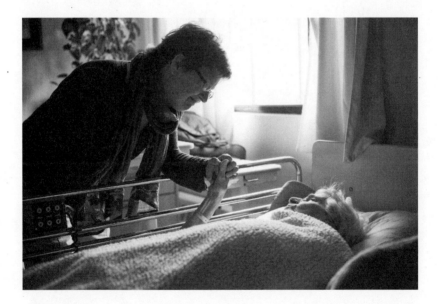

When interested
how vital life becomes!

Without interest or relationships
apathy sets in
I wander down life's path
cynical
and sad
sad unto death
how quickly I die
I fear my own violence.

Who will confront my violence
with tenderness?

Who will call me forth
and heal my brokenness
transform me
and lead me into celebration?

Feeling down
no vitality
no beauty
that beauty which flows with life
eyes
no radiance
no longer a source of attraction
people turn away
I am not only dejected
but rejected
covered with shame
humiliated
abandoned
alone in anguish
broken.

Dejected
I let go that inner hold
and sink down
down
friends drift by
laughing
I remain...lying on my bed
smoking
drinking
or sitting...sitting
the TV playing on and on and on
I am waiting
waiting
but waiting for what...?

I am afraid . . .
your haggard eyes
open wounds
black skin or white skin
alcoholic smell
addicted mind
I am afraid.

Your brokenness reminds me
of my own brokenness
of my own wounds
of my own violence
I flee
lest I recognize
myself
in you
my own wounds
in yours.

Your misery
strikes deep chords of fear within me . . .
fear of losing money, time, reputation, liberty
fear, above all, of losing myself
fear of the unknown,
for misery is a world of the unknown . . .
the terror of despair,
your hands . . .
your hands outstretched
towards
me . . .
I am afraid to touch them . . .
they may drag me down, down,
down into some unknown
brokenness within me . . .

I fear my own helplessness
my emptiness
my vulnerability
you remind me that I too must die
and so I turn my back
returning to the comfort of my life,
escaping the fundamental reality
of my own existence,
of my own fragility,
and of yours,
I refuse love...

I fear your grasping hand
calling me to the unknown
the unknown of love
because I fear my emptiness
my fragility
the call to my own death
I fear myself
I close my heart
rigid with fear...
shut myself off
from you,
my despairing brother, sister
you are in a prison of despair, sadness...
I too am in prison
but my bars and locks
are my so-called friends, clubs, social conventions,
"what everybody else is doing"...
barriers that I have built
that prevent me seeing you,
my brother, my sister
your presence,
miserable, sad, isolated...
is a call...
do I turn away
or do I dare...?
Love is the greatest of all risks
to give myself...to you
do I dare...do I dare
leap into the risky, swirling, living waters
of loving fidelity.

The person in misery still waits . . .
waiting . . .
waiting for what?

Lying in a prison
of pain and self loathing
waiting
· yet
not waiting
having lost all hope
we only wait when there is hope
where there is no hope . . . we lie . . . dying
not living
sad unto death
waiting . . . yet not waiting.

The miserable person
without hope
not ignorant
only lacking in energy, vitality
which spring from hope
when there is no hope...

The misery is greater because of this awareness
therein lies despair and anguish
not feeling worthy of rising
unable to rise.

The person in misery does not need a look that
judges and criticizes
but a comforting presence
that brings peace and hope and life
which says:
"you are a human person
important
mysterious
infinitely precious
what you have to say
is important
because it flows
from a human person
in you there are those seeds
of the infinite
those seeds of love, of beauty
which must rise up from the earth
of your misery
so humanity may be fulfilled.

If you do not rise
then something will be missing
rise again
because we all need you
for you are a child of God
my brother, my sister
be loved
beloved
and we can walk together."

In some mysterious way
the quality of my presence, my look
brings life to you
and I too am transformed
or death
for us both.

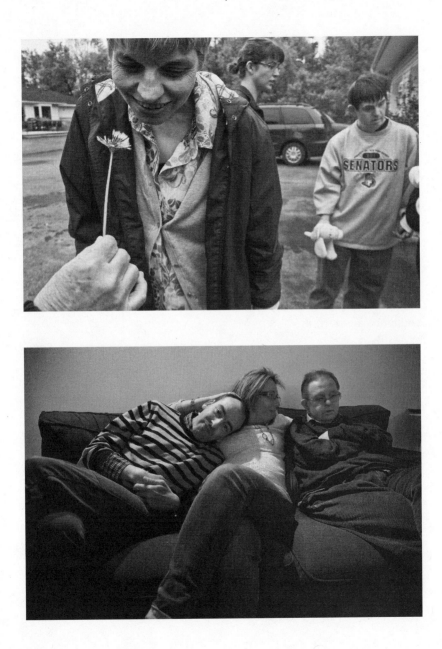

Your look...
your hand...
call forth
life...hope...joy...
if
you believe in me
then maybe
I can do something worthwhile...
maybe I am worthwhile
maybe I can do something with my life
thus
the light of hope begins to shine
your faithful presence
and constant trust in me
communicate warmth
and faith
the look in your eyes
the touch of your hands
bring me a marvellous message of hope
disarm me
unfold me.

your slightest look easily will unclose me
though I have closed myself as fingers,
you open always petal by petal myself as Spring opens
(touching skilfully, mysteriously) her first rose

       e. e. cummings

How then to approach the wounded person?

Lovingly
humbly
not from above
but from below
not dominating
not giving things
rather giving myself
my time
my energy
my listening
my heart
my belief
that each person is important
a child of God
touching gently
tenderly offering friendship
delicate soothing hands
bearing the oil of mercy
anointing deep wounds.

A new heart will I give you
and a new spirit I will put within you
and I will take out of your flesh the heart of stone
and give you a heart of flesh.

Ezekiel 36:26

He who is
or has been
deeply hurt
has a RIGHT
to be sure
he is
LOVED.

Love!

Not just some passing moment
nor a glance, however open
but a deeper compassion
radiating permanence
not some morbid curiosity
or gushing pity
or kind charity
or incompetent naïveté.
The call of burnt-out eyes
wounded bodies
addicted minds
cravings
can only be answered by a deeper love
unswerving
growing gently
in which is felt the presence of the eternal
a hope
a new security
is born.

Compassion
is a meaningful word...
sharing the same passion
the same suffering
the same agony
accepting in my heart
the misery in yours, o, my brother, my sister,
and with your acceptance of me
I dare to accept myself.

Oh yes, there is fear
but more deeply
there is the insistent cry from the heart of suffering
which calls me forth...
some faint feeling
of trust
that my smile...my presence
has value
and can give life.

Thus friendship is born
communion
mutual presence
humble and forgiving
engendering
quiet joy
fidelity.

Who will bring life
to the despairing,
to crushed and dying hearts
to those whose future is empty
to those sick in mind or spirit
to the very old and alone
to the despised and anguished
to the burnt out?

Statesmen are called to enact laws
but who is called to give hope to the despairing?

How with my fear and my security can I approach the one
who repulses me?

Yet I feel...
in some mysterious way
there is a calling
the silent crying out of misery
tears of silence
and in my deepest being I hear this call
a whispering
that life has meaning,
but only to the degree
that I find love
no reasons...
no explanation why...
only an intuition
a call of faith
that I can enter into some vast and powerful
movement
of life and life-giving.

A growing belief
that my joy gives joy
my hope gives hope
and
that I can communicate in some silent way
the Spirit living within me
not by what I say
but by the way I say it
a deep concern
a tender presence
a way of listening
to the faint heartbeats
of your existence and life.

For this, I need community
I need others
to hold and confirm me
to call me to prayer and faithfulness
in listening to and responding to the cry
people bonded in love
born for a mission
to give life.

Together
listening
listening to the whispers
from the heart of suffering
silently
a listening that comforts
and calls forth.

DO I DARE
do we dare
believe
hear your silent call
welcome your tears of silence?

There exists the world of efficiency
computers, iPhones, diplomas
hierarchies of the elite
a world which creates few winners and many losers.

There remain my friends
who think I'm crazy . . .

Are they friends
am I crazy?
DOUBTS . . .
conflicting forces
fatigue, fears.

In spite of this strange and silent war
life persistently calls forth
the compassion of my deepest self
do I dare
do we dare
believe
and surrender ourselves to your call?

If you pour yourself out for the hungry
and satisfy the afflicted
then shall your light rise in the darkness
and your gloom be as the noonday
and the Lord will guide you continually
and you shall be like a watered garden
like a spring of water
whose water fail not.

Isaiah 58:10–11

O God
my God
keep me from flinching or waning,
from slumbering into that timeless rest
that never revitalizes
keep me from falling into a prison
of egotistical habits
where the barriers
of superficiality prevent life evolving
towards that taste of the infinite
open to your call...
break down those barriers
that prevent me living, my God,
break down those barriers
that threaten to stifle me...

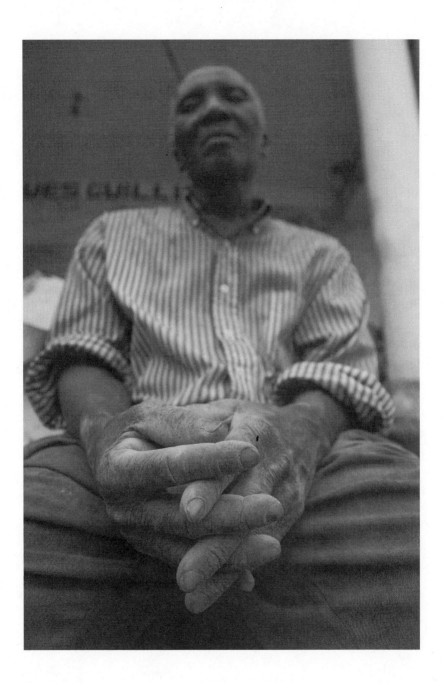

Barriers broken down too quickly
are
another form
of death...
too much exposure
those who seek escape too quickly
lose life
those who throw themselves into
experiences of addiction
sexuality
drugs to forget
lose life.

Presence
communion
and love grow gently
they spring forth
from a deepening union of peace
and liberty.

I fear
the mysterious power of compassion
compassion requires that I have found myself
and no longer
play the game
of putting on a mask, a personage
pretending to be
appearing.

Compassion requires
that I become myself
accepting my poverty
letting the Spirit breathe
move
live
love
in me
opening my being
without fear
to the delicate touch
of God's hand
accepting that I am loved
as I am
with my fears and frailties
with my intelligence and competencies
with my heart and with my hopes
free to be myself.

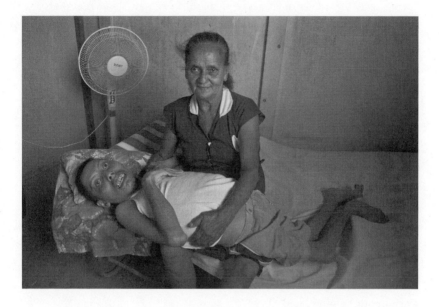

Maturity of the heart:
accepting
myself
with my limits
in my weaknesses
I no longer fear
the other who is broken and in misery
I no longer fear that
I will be eaten up
burnt out
lose my being
frightened
of revealing who I am.

I need your helping hand
gentle presence
so that I do not flinch or fall
or abandon the path of love.

In each of us there is a need to
LIVE
the flowering of life
the thirst for beautiful things
the feel of my radiance
in joy
in hope.

In each of us
there are the seeds of life
but also seeds of death
no will to live
no desire to get up in the morning
never able to sleep...
always wanting to sleep...
but never sleeping
always down
criticizing
blaming others
no zest or energy
living a taste of death
in quiet desperation.

I need to feel
I am
I am unique
capable of love and life
recognized and appreciated
not just a bystander
but rather an eager and welcome participant
fully alive
fully human
dancing with humanity.

Life is a flowering vine...
too much light... or too little
too much water... or too little
brings blight and death... burnt-up, dried up, drowned...

Life longs for delicate gentle hands,
hands that know
just the right amount of water for growth
just the right degree of light
at the right moment.

We are each part of a beautiful planet earth
where all life is called to grow, flower, and bear fruit.

To evolve
life needs the security
of a family
of a home
of friends
a community of brothers and sisters
trusting in the Spirit
strength
against assaults of fear and anguish
against all the unknowns
against anything that threatens
the flowering of life...

The biological movement
of growth
needs
this physical and spiritual
complement of love.

To evolve
the child
needs security
competent care
looks of tenderness
hands of love.

Life needs
the fundamental security
of the womb, the earth
in which life is conceived, born, and nutured
then, the breaking through into light
the breath of air
love
beauty
universality
whispers of the infinite.

Risk
and hope
love of the unknown
passionate interest in the present
thirst for adventure
desire for new experiences
outpourings of generosity
quest for knowledge
openness to the future
call to love
availability to the Spirit
peaceful contemplation
prayerful listening
high skies
mountains
deep lakes
deep breathing
wonderment.

Love is the greatest of all risks
the giving of myself
do I dare take this risk
diving into the cool
swirling
living waters of
LOVING FIDELITY.

An encounter
is a strange
and wonderful thing
presence
one person to another
present
one to another
life flowing
one to another.

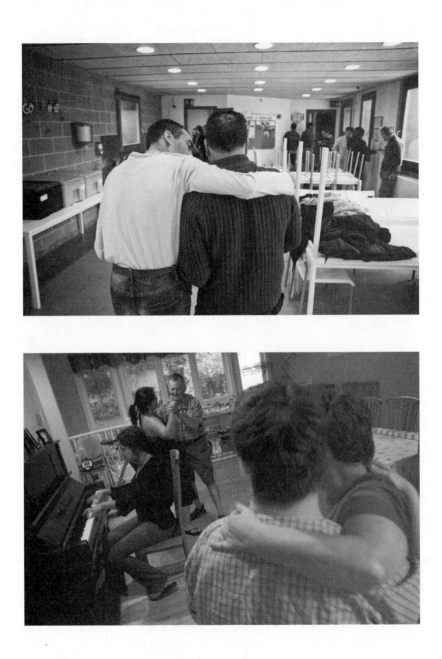

We can be together
and not meet
we can live in the same house day after day
sit at the same table
kneel at the same pew
read the same books
communicate
through phone and email
but never meet
we can kiss
gestures of love
apparent tenderness
but never meet.

To meet we must listen
listen intently
my God I wish I could listen
to you, my brother, my sister,
listen to your faint heartbeats
listen to those faint ... o so faint ...
calls
which are there
hidden
under ...

I know not why ...
your fear
listening
do I dare?

But instead
I dominate
and destroy
the fragile trust.

I remain
isolated
stagnating
in quiet desperation.

I need to talk
and walk
with another
a friend
I need to express myself
say things
and welcome life from another
live in truth
this is the movement of life
life that is in me and in you
needing to flow out...

I must speak...and dance
sharing things I love and hate
my hopes, my joys, my fears, my griefs, my weaknesses...

Giving myself
giving my life
giving life
receiving yours
living communion.

Always
our hearts are like children.

A tiny child needs not only food and shelter
but something more ... much more ...
the certitude of being loved
of knowing that
someone really cares
ready to make sacrifices.

If the child is really loved
seen as important ... precious
then life rises up within and begins to flow
so the child grows in trust
and in potential
a marvelous part of creation.

Life-giving energy
conceived...
born...
and nurtured
in love.

I treat misery as a stranger.

You were born and reared
in squalor...
you are bereft
without opportunities ahead of you...
without joys to look forward to...
no loving children
no esteem.

I, with my clean clothes,
my sensitive nose
(I hate bad smells)
my politeness...
a warm house...
a world of security...

The light of reality
does not penetrate my cell,
the reality of human misery
so widespread, so deep...

We are as two prisoners
segregated from each other
the person in misery...
and, imprisoned in the cell next door,
the person of means
comfortably installed...
ever thus the world continues,
the gulf widens
who will be the bridge?

I do not want to be reborn
but if that should happen
I would like to find myself amongst the untouchables
in order to share their affliction,
their sufferings
and the insults they are subject to,
in this way,
perhaps I would have the chance
to liberate them and myself
from this miserable condition.

    Gandhi

Two worlds that never meet
divided by a gulf called fear...
who can assuage this fear
who can heal the wounds
riches will not bring comfort
to those without hope...
they need the warm light of a trusting relationship
which calls forth their blessedness.

Familiar with their misery
convinced of their
apparent worthlessness
they are not lacking knowledge
but rather the hope and strength
to rise from the depths...
where to find this strength
which springs from hope
and a relationship which conquers despair?

Who will hear
the silent cry
rising from the prisons
the psychiatric wards
the red light districts
and all those slum areas of our world
from all those who are humiliated,
lonely and broken?

Blessed are the merciful
for they shall obtain mercy.

Jesus

PHOTO CAPTIONS

Duékoué,
Ivory Coast, 2012

Duékoué,
Ivory Coast, 2012

Toronto, Canada,
2013

Toronto, Canada,
2013

Toronto, Canada,
2013

Bouaké, Ivory Coast,
2012

Québec, Canada,
2013

Toronto, Canada,
2013

Toronto, Canada,
2013

Tegucigalpa,
Honduras, 2011

Bouaké, Ivory Coast,
2012

Toronto, Canada,
2013

Bouaké, Ivory Coast,
2012

Cayes, Haiti, 2009

Port-au-Prince, Haiti,
2008

Bonoua, Ivory Coast,
2012

Malmö, Sweden,
2013

Arnprior, Canada,
2010

Tordera, Spain, 2013

Toronto, Canada,
2013

Tordera, Spain, 2013

Tordera, Spain, 2013

Trosly-Breuil, France,
2012

Ottawa, Canada,
2010

Bonoua, Ivory Coast,
2012

Port-au-Prince, Haiti,
2008

Toronto, Canada,
2013

Québec, Canada,
2013

Port-au-Prince, Haiti,
2010

Bouaké, Ivory Coast,
2012

Choluteca,
Honduras, 2011

Montréal, Canada,
2009

Duékoué, Ivory Coast, 2012   Port-au-Prince, Haiti, 2010   Chantal, Haiti, 2008   Bouaké, Ivory Coast, 2012

Tegucigalpa, Honduras, 2011   Lobimo, Ivory Coast, 2012   Tegucigalpa, Honduras, 2011   Cayes, Haiti, 2011

Tordera, Spain, 2013   Bouaké, Ivory Coast, 2012   Duékoué, Ivory Coast, 2012   Tordera, Spain, 2013

Ottawa, Canada, 2010   Tordera, Spain, 2013   Tegucigalpa, Honduras, 2011   Toronto, Canada, 2013

Tegucigalpa, Honduras, 2011   Katiola, Ivory Coast, 2012   Cayes, Haiti, 2011   Toronto, Canada, 2013

Gonaives, Haiti, 2008   Gonaives, Haiti, 2008   Tegucigalpa, Honduras, 2011

ACKNOWLEDGEMENTS

My thanks to Martha Bala, who worked on the text, making it more truthful and loving, and to Isabelle Aumont, Director of the Jean Vanier Association, whose faithful and loving persistence has pulled the whole project along and the actors together, and without whom this revised edition would not be in our hands today.

— Jean Vanier

ACKNOWLEDGEMENTS

My first acknowledgements go to Olivier, the man who welcomed me in a community and became my friend when I still didn't know what true friendship was. We do not see each other often, but you are always in my heart.

To my family and friends for continuously believing in my dreams.

To *moineau*, for teaching me so much about life, righteousness, and the wind.

To Margaret Williamson, the most inspiring photo-editor I have had the privilege to meet.

To the many L'Arche communities around the world for welcoming me with kindness and love.

And finally, to every person I have ever met along the way. I have failed at giving each one of you the true attention and time you deserve, but your lives have changed the way I see this world, and want to act in it.

— Jonathan Boulet-Groulx

ABOUT THE AUTHORS

Jean Vanier is the son of former Governor General of Canada Georges Vanier, and founder of L'Arche, an international network of communities for people with developmental disabilities. He has written a number of books, including *Becoming Human*, the 1999 CBC Massey Lectures, *Made for Happiness*, a national bestseller, and *Finding Peace*. Jean Vanier lives in Trosly-Breuil, France.

Jonathan Boulet-Groulx is a photographer based in Montreal, Quebec. Visit his website at www.mwenpafou.org.